The Pandemic Cancelled it, and They Never Brought it Back:

STORIES OF LOSS, CHANGE, AND HOPE

KARLA AUSDERAU and JENNIFER CAPELLE

Copyright © 2025 Karla Ausderau and Jennifer Capelle

All rights reserved. No part of this publication may be reproduced, distributed, or transmitted in any form or by any means, including photocopying, recording, digital scanning, or other electronic or mechanical methods, without the prior written permission of the publisher, except in the case of brief quotations embodied in critical reviews and certain other noncommercial uses permitted by copyright law. For permission requests or other information, please send correspondence to the following address:

Little Creek Press
5341 Sunny Ridge Road
Mineral Point, WI 53565

ORDERING INFORMATION
Quantity sales. Special discounts are available on quantity purchases by corporations, associations, and others. For details, contact info@littlecreekpress.com

Printed in the United States of America

Cataloging-in-Publication Data
Names: Karla Ausderau and Jennifer Capelle
Title: The Pandemic Cancelled It, and They Never Brought it Back
Description: Mineral Point, WI Little Creek Press, 2025
ISBN: 978-1-955656-86-3

Book design by Little Creek Press

Acknowledgments

We extend our heartfelt gratitude to the incredible individuals who have allowed us into their lives to share their unique perspectives and experiences. Your strength and resilience have brought the pages of this book to life. This project would not have been possible without the dedication and enthusiasm of each of you.

We would also like to express our appreciation for the families, care partners, and support networks that have played a crucial role in making this project a reality. You have been instrumental in bringing these powerful narratives to light.

We would like to acknowledge our amazing research and data collection team for their hard work and dedication. Their commitment to ensuring the authenticity and integrity of the participants' stories has been invaluable.

Funding: This work was supported by the Wisconsin Partnership Program Partnership, Education, and Research Committee COVID19 Response Grant (AAJ8474) and in part by a core grant to the Waisman Center from the Eunice Kennedy Shriver National Institute of Child Health and Human Development (P50HD105353).

Dedication

We dedicate this book to those whose voices remain unheard. Your strength inspires us, your memory lives on, and your absence is deeply felt. May this collection of images stand as a tribute to your silent narratives and unseen struggles. Your presence, resilience, and spirit endure as a profound reminder of the challenges faced by so many during the COVID-19 pandemic.

We also recognize the strength of those who have navigated disruptions in their daily routines, faced isolation, and encountered unprecedented difficulties. People with intellectual and developmental disabilities felt the impact of the COVID-19 pandemic in many unique and exacerbated ways, resulting in their needs going unmet. May this book serve as a testament to the courage and adaptability demonstrated by the community of individuals with intellectual and developmental disabilities whose daily lives continue to be impacted.

A very special thank you to the artists at ArtWorking who contributed their art to this project!

Artworking.org

Cover art: Rose Hefling: "Bursting Free"

Page 8: Nick Bursh: "NEED TITLE"

Page 10: Heather Sarabia: "Force My Hand"

Page 14: Rose Hefling: "Bursting Free"

Page 16: Barb Priem: "Houses and Lakes and Peoples"

Page 34: Hope Lane: "Doctor Who"

Page 45: Joe Wahlers: "NEED TITLE"

Page 46: Briana Richardson: "Please Come Join Me on My Walk"

Page 63: Jacob Bultman: "NEED TITLE"

Page 64: Lainey Singer: "Bold Colorful Skeleton"

Page 74: Romano Johnson: "The Yellow Moon Healing God"

Page 79: Hope Lane: "The Orange Moon"

ArtWorking is a Madison area nonprofit program that provides career development and support for artists & entrepreneurs with disabilities.

KARLA AUSDERAU • JENNIFER CAPELLE

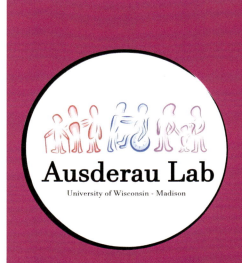

The Ausderau Lab is focused on improving the health and well-being of individuals with intellectual and developmental disabilities and their families. Dr. Ausderau's research considers the individual, family, caregiving community, and the person's environment when looking at a person's development and well-being. The Ausderau Lab uses diverse research methods to better understand neurodiversity, intellectual and developmental disabilities, and disease processes and their effect on an individual's development, engagement in meaningful occupations, and community engagement. Dr. Ausderau is also invested in inclusive research, elevating the voices and goals of the people and communities that her research focuses on. The Ausderau Lab collaborates with students, trainees, clinicians, university researchers, researchers with lived experience, individuals, and organizations to maintain accountability to the communities involved in the research.

This book was made possible through the hard work and dedication of many individuals including the Ausderau Lab, research partners with lived experience, and community partners.

Karla Ausderau, PhD, OTR, FAOTA
Role: Principal Investigator
Favorite COVID Activity: Hanging out with my husband and son

Jennifer Capelle, OTD
Role: Project Lead
Favorite COVID Activity: Trying to bake fancy desserts

With Significant Contribution From

LIBBY HLADIK, OTR
Role: Senior Project Assistant
Favorite COVID Activity: Zooming with my parents and siblings

CLARE WANGLER
Role: Junior Project Assistant
Favorite COVID Activity: Hiking

JADYN SCHENSKY
Role: Junior Project Assistant
Favorite COVID Activity: Family walks with my dog

ALLISON CAUDILL, OTR
Role: WPP Project Assistant
Favorite COVID Activity: Reading

MARQUIS GARNER
Role: Research Partner with Lived Experience
Favorite COVID Activity: Praying with my grandma

EDWARD KASTERN
Role: Research Partner with Lived Experience
Favorite COVID Activity: Online theatre classes

A special thank you to: Sabrina Kabakov, Hannah Laufenburg, Aubre Poole, Stephanie Shoaf, Rachel Spanton, Brittany St. John

Table of Contents

9	Foreword
11	Introduction
12	Glossary
12	Context Definitions
13	How Does Photo Voice Work
15	Change
17	Home
35	Work
47	Community
65	Health
75	Spirituality & Beliefs

Nick Bursh—Labyrinth

NICK BURSH

Nick is an artist that draws from real life and also from his imagination. He loves the use of colors and bright images to show how the world shines in his mind. He loves to paint with circles and lines mixed with the bright colors to symbolize looking through a stained glass to the outside life. My mind is like that stained glass and I invite the viewer to gaze Inside.

Foreword

Beth Swedeen
Executive Director of the Wisconsin Board for People with Developmental Disabilities

The old saying "a picture is worth a thousand words" is especially true for people who often struggle to make their voices heard. People living with intellectual and developmental disabilities can be overlooked and undervalued in our society. Yet communities are all richer when the insights, perspectives and experiences of people with disabilities are elevated and understood. And visual representation can be one of the most effective tools for sharing the stories, experiences and contributions that people with disabilities offer. People with disabilities have much to contribute, as this book demonstrates through the beautiful photos captured by its authors: stories of their jobs, their families and friends, and their favorite activities. All of these connections were abruptly disrupted during COVID-19, and many never returned. In this book, people with disabilities share how rich their lives were, what was lost, and how they are processing those losses: all through their own photos with captions they created. That such a deeply insightful and poignant book can also serve as a vehicle to further research on the long-term impacts of the pandemic is also due to the unique contributions of the book's authors: who came together as visual artists, storytellers, and ultimately as researchers. This may be the best "research paper" you ever see...and read!

Edward Kastern & Marquis Garner

As researchers with disabilities, we work to make sure that our voices and the voices of others with disabilities are heard not only within our community, but by people in key positions like healthcare, government, and education. Our work as researchers helps to improve the lives of others with disabilities; to give them more rights, more access, more freedom. As an African American autistic man, being a researcher gives me the chance to be a voice for people with disabilities and also for our minority community. There are a lot of people who may not have a voice and as a father and a person with cerebral palsy who uses a wheelchair, I am able to use my voice to advocate for people who share my experience. We want to empower people with disabilities to have confidence, to know that they are important, that they have something to say, that their lives are valuable. We are working towards change. Change for a generation of people with disabilities.

This book will open doors for a lot of different audiences to better understand what people with disabilities went through on a daily basis during the COVID-19 pandemic. We see this book as a way to help improve their futures, to make it brighter, to give opportunities like employment equality and equal access to healthcare. We see this book as a starting point for a conversation with people with disabilities. We hope these conversations will educate others and lead to change. We are working to improve the lives of people with disabilities so they can live enjoyable, healthy lives without having to worry because they know all their needs are met. We just want people with disabilities to be able to dream and to live in harmony and peace like everyone else in our communities!

Force my hand I will bite back
Problem only is my realization
to kick until the robbers of dignity leaders
know that I can perceive my own destiny

Poorly planned policies
good fire for change

Heather Sarabia—Force My Hand

HEATHER SARABIA

I didn't choose to become an artist, I am one.

My art is a point of grounding for me.

Art gives my lonely heart the purpose to move forward.

My favorite part of being an artist is going to art shows and seeing people smile.

I can express my treatment by society because of my autism through my art.

Heather Sarabia was a painter and poet with autism. She developed her paintings through sweeping motions, creating layers of brush strokes rich with movement and gesture.

Introduction

Photovoice is a unique research method based on the theories of empowerment, feminism, and documentary photography. The Photovoice method is intended to be used to stimulate conversations around community issues and initiate changes in policy to improve social justice.[1] Focused on highlighting the voices of people who have been marginalized, Photovoice offers an expression of the human experience and creates research opportunities for participants who have been excluded. People with intellectual and developmental disabilities (IDD) have historically been a population excluded from research. Photovoice is an effective data collection method with people who have communication and/or cognitive differences, such as those with intellectual and developmental disabilities.[2] In using Photovoice, the participants are able to decide how their experiences are depicted through their photos with captions to help share their stories. By utilizing the photos and words that they used to describe them, others are able to better understand their lived experiences.

The global reach of the COVID-19 pandemic touched the lives of everyone in the world. We have heard and seen stories from so many people about the impact it had. People with Intellectual and developmental disabilities were not given the same opportunity to share their stories. They were not considered in the policies that were put into place. Their work, social life, and daily routines were very much affected and still are to this day.

Using Photovoice as a method for our research study, we explored the daily occupations of 18 adults with Intellectual and developmental disabilities in Wisconsin during the COVID-19 pandemic. People with intellectual and developmental disabilities already experience disparities in access and participation; safety precautions throughout the pandemic further limited their ability to access and participate in meaningful occupations.[3] These photos and narratives have a depth and complexity that necessitated dissemination beyond the typical research manuscript. From that need, this book was born.

1 Wang, C., & Burris, M. A. (1994). Empowerment through Photo Novella: Portraits of Participation. *Health Education Quarterly, 21*(2), 171–186. https://doi.org/10.1177/109019819402100204

2 St. John, B., Gray, M., Malzacher, A., Hladik, L., Lurie, S., & Ausderau, K. (2021). Using photovoice with people with intellectual disability to illuminate definitions of health and factors influencing participation in health promotion. *Journal of Applied Research in Intellectual Disabilities, 34*(3), 866–876. https://doi.org/10.1111/jar.12868

3 Courtenay, K., & Perera, B. (2020). COVID-19 and people with intellectual disability: Impacts of a pandemic. *Irish Journal of Psychological Medicine, 37*(3), 231–236. https://doi.org/10.1017/ipm.2020.45

Glossary

Authenticity: how real or accurate something is

COVID-19 Pandemic: represents a period of time in which a dangerous virus spread rapidly around the world. For this book, we are considering that time period to be March 2020-October 2022 when the photos were taken

Disparities: differences or inequalities

Dissemination: sharing information or spreading awareness

Empowerment: gaining power

Exacerbated: making something that is already bad even worse

Feminism: belief that women deserve equal rights

Integrity: being honest and trustworthy

Marginalized: groups of people who are being treated unfairly and as if they are not important

Resilience: ability to overcome and adapt to things that are hard

Stimulate: to encourage, start, or motivate

Unprecedented: never before seen or experienced

Context Definitions

The context of the photos and captions were based on what was included in the image and how it was described in the caption. Photos and captions were grouped into the contexts of Home, Work, Community, and Healthcare that aligned with the original prompts the participants were given as part of the research question. A fifth context also became evident, Spirituality, that went beyond the original context categories.

How Does PhotoVoice Work

ORIENTATION
People reviewed the study and gave consent. They met the research team and brainstormed ideas of which pictures they wanted to take and where.

TAKE PICTURES
Each person picked two locations to take pictures. The research partner met with them and assisted with taking pictures, if needed.

WRITE CAPTIONS
Research partners asked questions about each photo: 1) Why was the picture taken? 2) What is happening in the picture? 3) What does it tell us about your experience?

FOCUS GROUPS
People met in small groups with peers and research partners to talk about their pictures and experiences.

ANALYSIS
The research team looked at pictures, captions, and transcripts of focus groups to find common themes among the pictures and the conversations.

ACTION
The research team used the pictures and captions to create this photobook to ensure the stories were shared with others to educate people and inform change.

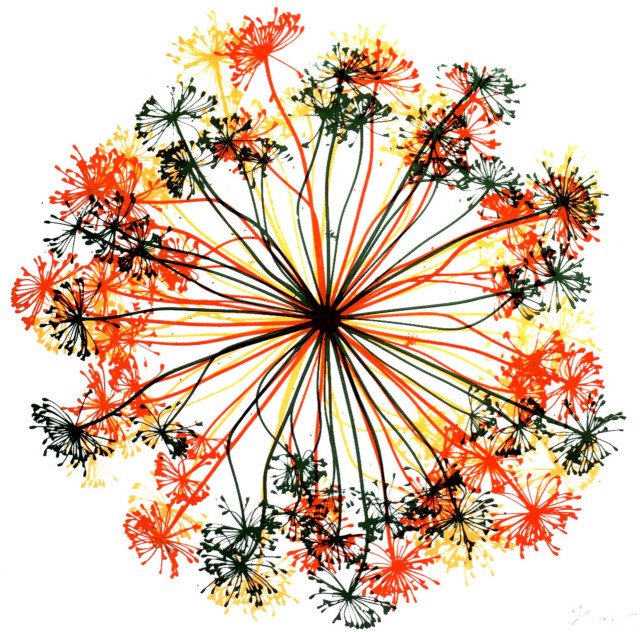

Rose Hefling—Bursting Free

ROSE HEFLING

Originally from rural southern Kentucky, I spent the first part of my childhood running wild and free, barefoot, in the countryside, and the resulting love of nature compelled me to major in Environmental Studies at Beloit College. I later studied botany as part of the Agroecology Master's Program at UW-Madison, and while my OCD kept me from completing the program, there is no such thing as a reformed botanist. Consequently, this long standing love of nature and flora leads me to frequently incorporate plants into my artwork.

While art and Nature have always been important to me, it has become apparent in recent years that they are two of the only arenas in which I can successfully tackle the severe, treatment-resistant OCD that has plagued me since childhood. Unlike traditional treatment modalities, art provides adequate motivation for me to ignore my obsessions and overcome my compulsions, albeit temporarily, and I simply feel safe and at peace in Nature. Attempting to adequately capture Nature's infinite beauty is a never ending challenge that I thoroughly enjoy, and I hope that my reverence shines through in my work.

Change

Family
Technology
Must keep others safe!

Things I missed
New activities
A different way of doing things...

Barb Priem—Houses and Lakes and People

BARB PRIEM

Barb Priem creates complex landscapes, cityscapes, and other environments with a variety of mediums.

"I draw different objects and shapes using colored pencils, pens, watercolor, and gouache. I love using greens, reds, blues, and pinks most of all. I also do large collage pictures with my drawings."

Priem often works in amixed-media layers to create original works as well as her signature one-of-a-kind cards.

"Art makes me feel like I'm doing something good for other people."

Home

Staying healthy at home

Being with family

Activities done at home to pass the time

Home as location, stuck there

When the center closed, I walked this path on and off but not as much as I do now.

Top left: Where I was during lockdown.

Top right: Spent a lot of time in my house in COVID. Stayed distanced. I had to keep my roommates safe. Wore a mask at home and stayed in my room a lot.

Bottom: To show that I existed there. Lived there 40 years before moving out. Walked driveway during Covid for physical activity. Lived there for a long time and moved out 9 months ago.

THE PANDEMIC CANCELLED IT, AND THEY NEVER BROUGHT IT BACK

When I was living with my parents we all were living together—my siblings and I, and my parents were all living together. It was hard sometimes.

Inset: I moved out and I became more independent.

I am at my house waiting for the day to get started. I like to be outside. Being at home is kind of boring. How much I had to stay home. It was all the time. I got tired of it. I think everybody did get tired of being home.

It is meaningful at my house. I was home more than normal.

THE PANDEMIC CANCELLED IT, AND THEY NEVER BROUGHT IT BACK

I read a lot during lockdown. I read a lot because I couldn't go anywhere.

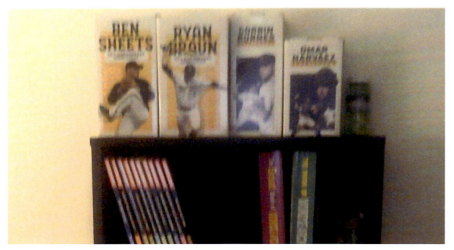

I did a lot of activities and reading. Was another opportunity to read and keep our minds off the bad stuff.

I am a gamer. It is soothing for me and calms me down. If I didn't have nothing to do, I would lose my mind in the pandemic.

Sitting around a table playing games. It is something we did at home when activities were canceled.

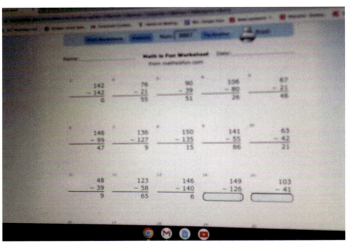

Top left: I started using [dad's] computer for Zoom, then my computer. I used Zoom to do [an activity] group. I learned how to be assertive and look for YouTube videos.

Top right and bottom: Started doing math, when COVID hit, did before COVID but did it more during. Learned to use time differently.

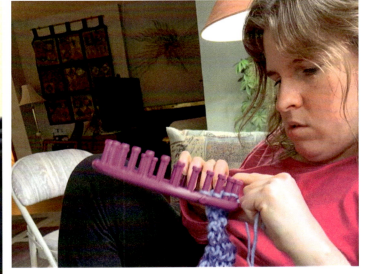

This picture shows me stuck at my parents house. This photo was taken when I was first learning how to knit. I am knitting a cup holder. When you get a drink from starbucks and get a sleeve, I'm making that, but prettier. Knitting is a new hobby that I learned how to do during the pandemic. I make scarves and leg warmers. I am selling them. I joined an artist studio.

THE PANDEMIC CANCELLED IT, AND THEY NEVER BROUGHT IT BACK

Working on my workbooks. I do them since the pandemic got started to keep my brain working.

I started playing piano during the pandemic – I needed new activities. I still play piano. I play Disney songs.

I help watch [him] when Mom is doing something. I started watching him after he was born in Spring 2021.

Something fun that I did during COVID. I started a year ago and I want to get a computer controller and learn how to fly.

I learned how to cook and bake, which increased during COVID. I took baked goods and treats to grandma and her friends. It was a hard realization that I couldn't give grandma a hug.

I never stopped baking and cooking. More than before the pandemic because we didn't go out to eat. Reminds me of how I baked when I was six.

Took a Zoom class on cooking. Making homemade pizza.

Cooking gives me something to do. I'm [an adult], I should be helping out. I cooked more during the pandemic because I was home all the time...staring at the wall.

Eat more at home during the pandemic. Dining out less.

Eat food, stay healthy. Cooked more meals at home. Used microwave more.

This is important to do dishes, don't want to get dirty. I have been doing some at home but I do more for a friend that I clean for.

Top left: I had my own bathroom, TV room, and bedroom when I had COVID. I quarantined twice. My mom thought it was nice. I still have long-COVID.

Bottom left: I watched a lot of TV during the pandemic when I couldn't go anywhere. I was bored and wanted to do something else. I did some puzzles while I watched TV.

Top right: I am a YouTube addict- I love TV. I started re-watching That 70's Show. I bought the whole box set. "There's nothing to do besides sit in the basement and be weird", what they're saying, I agree with.

Bottom right: Me sitting on the couch with my face plastered to TV watching soap opera. Since pandemic, when lived with aunt, I got hooked on soap opera. I started watching soap opera during pandemic.

TV is how I learned about COVID-19 virus. Church on TV. Watch any TV. TV inside room.

Kahoot is a fun and exciting activity. Used computer for a lot of stuff. Used the computer to TV to broadcast. It was stressful staying at home and not seeing staff. Did a lot at home.

I watched a lot of movies. It was a way of passing the time.

[Showing] how important technology is. Like, if the pandemic happened 10 years ago, how would any of this have been possible? I had to figure out technology. I had never used Zoom prior to the pandemic. I can't hear someone and I'm frustrated with the technology.

Stay in contact with your family so they know what's wrong with you, if you got it or not. It wasn't hard to stay in contact with them.

I take any messages, texts, pictures; in case I got sick. The phone would help you contact people.

THE PANDEMIC CANCELLED IT, AND THEY NEVER BROUGHT IT BACK

How I keep in contact with my family. I have to make sure they are still here. I lost some of my people in the pandemic.

Checking on people. Letting them know I am okay. Making sure loved ones are okay, too.

31

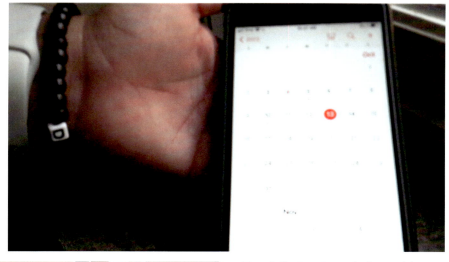

Top left: I'm Facetiming with friends because during the pandemic it was a way of staying connected. It wasn't the same as being in person, but it kept it somewhat normal.

Top right: Travel dates. No flying home by yourself during COVID. Hard to see family.

Bottom: I send at least one email a day. Helped me stay in contact with people.

She's my baby, my bundle of joy. Coco Chanel. I got her in the pandemic. My other cat, Tinker Bell, died during the pandemic.

My brother died and he is holding my cocker spaniel who passed. I was going through a period of depression after my dog and brother died. I was bored and needed something to do.

I'm wearing my brother's jacket. I feel special with it on. I didn't see him for a long time in the pandemic. He lives in Las Vegas.

HOPE LANE

"My name is Hope Lane and I am an artist with a passion to become a graphic designer. I'm on the autism spectrum and the way that I deal with my disability is through my art. I love to paint using acrylic colors on canvas and I love the feeling of picking up that brush and expressing myself and having that feeling of knowing that I am capable of anything. The colors I use are a symbol of how I see the world and how I want that world to look."

Hope Land—Doctor Who

Work

Changes in work, school, and volunteering

Gratitude for work

The stopping, waiting, and restarting of work activities

Still working [there]. I work events. The type of event changed, more funerals. And had to set up chairs distanced.

The place that I work. I worked there during COVID. I stock shelves and am a good person to talk to and show somewhere. I worked before, during, and after lockdown.

These are pans for serving catering. It reminds me of when I would go out and help serve catering. I helped homeless eat at the beginning of the pandemic. I still do this.

I'm a teacher and I love to teach. Teaching kids about how to stay close to God. I have good patience. I teach kids 3 and 4 years old.

Culver's had to hire more people. Raised wages—got a raise!

Culver's had to do curbside pickup

THE PANDEMIC CANCELLED IT, AND THEY NEVER BROUGHT IT BACK

I had to stock things differently at work. Ketchup pumps replaced with packets. Salt and pepper shakers replaced with packets.

Before the pandemic, I didn't have the opportunity to work from home and that all changed with the pandemic. Now I can work from home when needed. Working from home with so many others, my family, it was hard to find space.

I was in school. Better to be online than on campus so I don't get sick.

Doing virtual school on computer. Represents change moving from in person to online. You will have obstacles.

I like working in the kitchen in the Senior Center.

They had to close this down, I'm sorry it happened. I was sad when it stopped. I got my job back. I was lucky to get it back.

Putting to go order. More people do takeout than eat in. Eat takeout when restaurant closed. Procedures to keep customer safe.

Happy that I graduated. A lot of computer work. School was virtual, and I did not like it a lot. It was hard not having in person contact, but did have graduation in person.

Keep clean from COVID. Putting on gloves on Sunday to work with kids. One of the kids had COVID. During COVID I couldn't sit around the table with the kids.

THE PANDEMIC CANCELLED IT, AND THEY NEVER BROUGHT IT BACK

Some of the routes on the sign aren't running any more. They stopped over the course of the pandemic. I've had to either find other routes or find another way to get around.

It's how I get around, like to work. When everything started shutting down my parents weren't comfortable with me taking the bus. I got a ride from one of my parents every day. And after, I was able to get independence and was in charge of my own transportation.

Showed where I had to sit and wait. The bus came one time per hour. I had to relearn how to do the bus. I didn't want to wear a mask. Had to learn a new route. I had to build my confidence back about using the bus.

 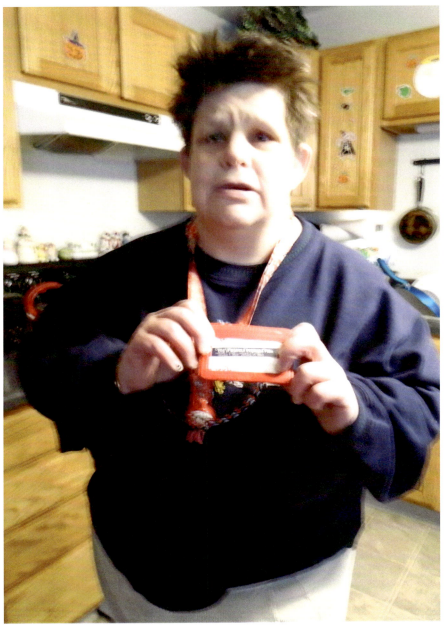

I like to ride the bus everyday to work. In the winter it is too slippery. I had to stop for a while and I didn't like it at all. I hate being at home.

THE PANDEMIC CANCELLED IT, AND THEY NEVER BROUGHT IT BACK

I spend a lot of time on the climber. We read books and communicate. I was happy to go back to work. There was 4 weeks of the pandemic when work was closed.

Me volunteering. When pandemic started, I stopped going to apartments for Meals on Wheels. I stopped volunteering at Second Harvest Food Bank.

Top left: I would meet and greet customers who come to Kwik Trip. I no longer worked when COVID started.

Top right: Used to work at Flix. Closed and couldn't work there anymore.

Bottom: This is where I worked before COVID. Closed during COVID and working there now again on Fridays. I left because of COVID, I didn't come here because of COVID. Gone for 2.5 years, but back now. My brother lived 2 blocks from here and took a job here because he was close and I could see my brother after work. It was hard to come back.

THE PANDEMIC CANCELLED IT, AND THEY NEVER BROUGHT IT BACK

On Fridays I used to go to volunteer at Gigi's playhouse in the morning and afternoon and I do these things instead to stay safe. I do that stuff because fun and it gives me something to do and it is my work.

My cleaning job. A friend needed help cleaning and I work to help pay for activities. I do this more now since I don't volunteer on Fridays because of pandemic, so now I work on Fridays.

JOE WAHLERS

Joe Wahlers creates abstract acrylic paintings that evoke landscapes and figures through organic, layered forms. Wahlers' distinctive style is present in each of their paintings and their process is inspired by their internal world as well as external influences such as fashion, theatre, and decor.

"My art is all about imagination. Imagination gives art its movement. It's very relaxing. I put beauty and spirituality in my paintings. It should be that way. I collect all my thoughts before I paint. It helps get all the emotions out. Art to create is beautiful – it gives the world something. Art is everywhere. You need art in every room. Headbands are the newest thing out. We are always creating more using our lovely fabric based on my paintings. They are something nice and full of color."

Joe Wahlers—A Mixture of Everything

BRIANA RICHARDSON

I am a deeply thoughtful acrylic and watercolor painter who works to create a spiritual and emotional experience for all viewers. The nature scenes I use as subject matter aim to create approachable and delightful images that audience members can bring their whole selves to. My hope is to create a unique experience for viewers where they can be inspired and lifted up. I have used art to find comfort in my own life and feel called to help provide that same comfort and light to others. Not only am I a talented painter, but I also use my caring and moving spirit in words. I am a dedicated poet who uses verse to encourage others to open their eyes and see the beauty around them. I am known for taking long walks where I spend time taking in the nature around me. I use these moments of openness and spirituality to inspire my work on the canvas as well as in text.

Throughout my life, I have turned to Ephesians 4:29 as a source of guidance. The words, "Let everything you say be good and helpful, so that your words will be an encouragement to those who hear you." have called me to use my art business to inspire hope and show the good in the world. You blessed me with the gift of ENCOURAGEMENT. You call me to encourage others to move towards you. You help me use my art, my writings, words, and verses to show one person, or only a handful of people, the joy of walking with you. I want to bring people's focus to the good in the world.

Briana Richardson—Please Come Join Me on My Walk

KARLA AUSDERAU • JENNIFER CAPELLE

Community

Staying in touch with technology

People, places, and things I missed

New activities

Top left: Bowling is my favorite sport and favorite things. It is a nice relaxing thing every Monday. It is important to keep bowling. During COVID we couldn't do it against other people, only in our [group].

Top right: Packers and Badgers bowling balls. Balls had to be wiped down.

Bottom: No high-fives. No handshakes. Arm bumps instead. Lane restrictions, masks during pandemic. Unified tournaments and location changes.

I liked watching the boxers. Saw this boxing place during COVID. Made me want to start boxing because of COVID.

Used to play bingo at bowling alley but moved to Zoom.

Had to distance when others playing pinball. Machines were wiped down.

During pandemic, Schoewgler's had to open up another room for social distancing. Also, masks!

THE PANDEMIC CANCELLED IT, AND THEY NEVER BROUGHT IT BACK

Spent time with my brother during COVID. Going to the library helped me get closer to my brother during COVID. Would wear masks when there.

Couldn't attend cousin's wedding as usual... but drove by, waved, and sang "Varsity".

Some things moved from in-person to online over Zoom during pandemic. Used phone to look up stuff and do Zoom meetings.

I like singing. I sing in the shower sometimes. We did choir on Zoom for a while. I like being back in person.

The Night to Remember event changed. It was brought to people's houses.

THE PANDEMIC CANCELLED IT, AND THEY NEVER BROUGHT IT BACK

I'm exercising using iPad. Used to do exercises in person, but Special Olympics moved to online classes for a while.

I got my Jays at Foot Locker and talked to girls at the mall. I could not do it during COVID.

I used to go to Spencers with friend to talk to girls. I stopped during COVID.

YMCA was closed during COVID.

They do African American hair. Wanted to get my hair done at the barber shop but they were closed during COVID. Hoping to go in the future.

Top left: Couldn't watch games in person.

Bottom left: Didn't get to watch Brewers games in 2020.

Top right: Latched- close baseball seat. Didn't get to watch Brewers games in 2020, then seats spaced apart.

THE PANDEMIC CANCELLED IT, AND THEY NEVER BROUGHT IT BACK

Top: I was taking a karaoke, dance, art, and Fantastic Friends classes. Since pandemic started, I had to find new opportunities. Gigi's closed for a year and half. No art or Fantastic Friends. Back in person. I'm happy they're open.

Bottom: Fantastic Friends (demonstrated by stuffed animals)

Couldn't dine in at fast food restaurants so had to eat in the car, or outside in [the] park. Missed dining in, talking to people, and getting free refills.

Couldn't go to preseason games during early months of pandemic.

I miss being outside the Union. I didn't get to go to the Union as much and I missed going.

I like the Hancock. I want to go back. I'm happy to see it again. I want to go back. I miss it.

THE PANDEMIC CANCELLED IT, AND THEY NEVER BROUGHT IT BACK

My metals from Special Olympics from around the world and back again. I got to do what I wanted to do. I met new friends and went all over the world. I loved doing this before the pandemic. I got 4 gold and I was jumping for joy.

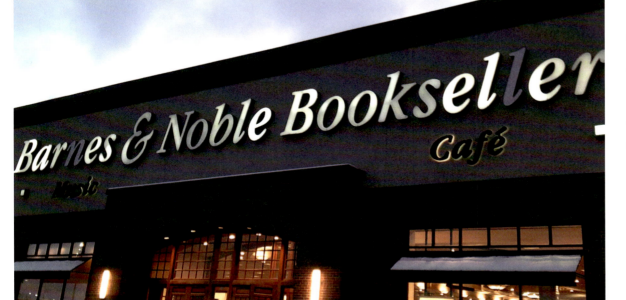

I was part of a book club at Barnes & Noble for adults with Intellectual and develompmental disabilities that met weekly. It was something I did for about 5 years every week and we stopped doing it when the pandemic started. It never started back up. I'm standing in the space where the book club met. I miss the people.

The pandemic canceled it, and they never brought it back.

Since pandemic got started and not doing special olympic bowling. It is fun for me. I still go bowling occasionally with friends and parents.

I'm standing in front of Planet Fitness. You can see the treadmills I used behind me. A home staff person took my housemate and me to Planet Fitness weekly to work out. We stopped going when the pandemic hit. During the pandemic, my home staff support person died, and I haven't wanted to go back to workout without [him] along.

I couldn't go to Y. When I'm upset, I like working out. I couldn't do that during COVID. Figured out how to workout at house.

My jersey for basketball & bowling. Couldn't compete during COVID. I love to cheer my teammate loud. We stay away from state [tournament]. COVID hit. Bad for all of us.

Middle of special olympics, swim team all canceled. Made me really sad to stop swimming.

I liked having fun at the Wheelhouse. I like doing it and it stopped during the pandemic. I still miss clay—I want to sign up for pottery classes.

No LOVinc events in person for at least a year after the pandemic and was looking for things to occupy my time.

THE PANDEMIC CANCELLED IT, AND THEY NEVER BROUGHT IT BACK

"It was significant in my life. During the pandemic, I walked with my mom down that way quite a bit."

KARLA AUSDERAU • JENNIFER CAPELLE

Going to the zoo is something I could not do during the pandemic. When the pandemic was happening I was living with my parents.

THE PANDEMIC CANCELLED IT, AND THEY NEVER BROUGHT IT BACK

Top: Nice relaxing place to sit next to during a down type of day, holy water in there brought back from Italy. Holy water comes out of angel mouth in fountain. In front of fountain is bench to sit at.

Bottom: Yellow, green, orange, red—COVID colors; seasons.

JACOB BULTMAN

Jacob Bultman divides his time in the studio between creating colorful paintings that are nearly totally abstract, and more representational work that reflects themes and interests that are important to him. Bultman also states that he gets inspiration for the work that he creates from "The things that I see in my head."

Jacob Bultman—All Seeing Eye

THE PANDEMIC CANCELLED IT, AND THEY NEVER BROUGHT IT BACK

LAINEY SINGER

Lainey Singer often works from reference photos and employs various media and techniques to create her signature designs. Her drawings, hand colored screen prints, and mixed media explorations are notable for their distinctive attention to detail and complex pattern work.

In her early work, Singer's drawings showed an already distinctive style, and tended toward illustrations of people with loose limbs, startling facial expressions, elaborately patterned clothing, and interesting poses. Early illustrations were evocative of the artwork of her grandfather, Gene Mandarino. Singer has continued to develop her signature style into a well crafted body of work that stretches across multiple genres and materials.

Singer's extraordinary gifts of visual perception and expression have been a source of inspiration, insight, and enjoyment to all who behold her work.

Lainey Singer—Bold Colorful Skeleton

KARLA AUSDERAU • JENNIFER CAPELLE

Health

Keeping self and others safe

Staying healthy

COVID-19 precautions

It was hard to get inserts because I couldn't get them in person.

Closer to family and friends by facetiming them. Doctor's appointments and other meetings or appointments. It was hard to communicate during COVID. It was hard to explain health concerns to doctors.

Signs were on the doors and no visitors used to be allowed. No visitors allowed, so-so impact. Not feel good. Had to wear masks everywhere. Made glasses fog up and hard to breathe.

Certain places wear mask to keep safe. School made me wear a mask. I wear it but it's hard to breathe in mask. Certain materials and textures I don't like. Had to wear mask at home in common space. Didn't like wearing a mask.

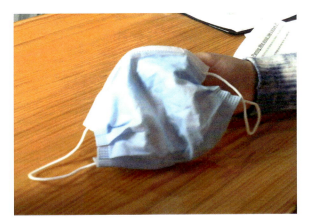

Covering your mouth cause of COVID. Wearing them on airlines during COVID. We had to wear masks at the doctor and nurses' office. And the dentist's office too. Wearing different masks to keep other people and ourselves safe. A series of different kinds of masks, some surgical, KN95, and N95. Sometimes they itched nose and mouth.

Social distancing and don't spread germs sign. Wear a mask sign. Wash hands sign. All signs about COVID-19. Tell us about it and what to do. Started at beginning of pandemic. Stay clean and get vaccinated.

Had to wear a mask when going to work, hospital, Special Olympics. It was not fun wearing a mask but helped protect from getting others sick.

THE PANDEMIC CANCELLED IT, AND THEY NEVER BROUGHT IT BACK

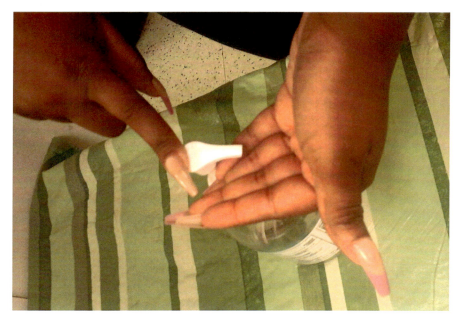

Purpose: You have to learn how to keep your hands clean. You have to protect yourself from getting COVID.

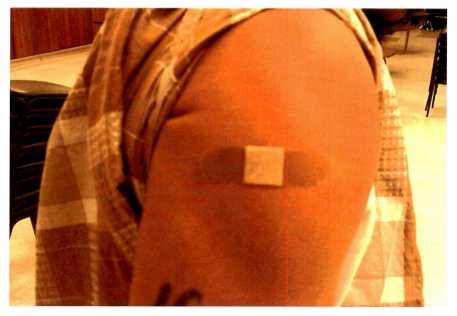

I got vaccinated to stay safe.

Dry your hands after you wash, more cleaning. Keep your hands clean.

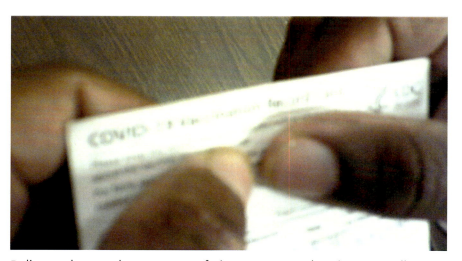

Policy and procedure to stay safe in COVID. I'm showing I got all my shots and booster shot to stay safe. Protect self from catching COVID at all costs.

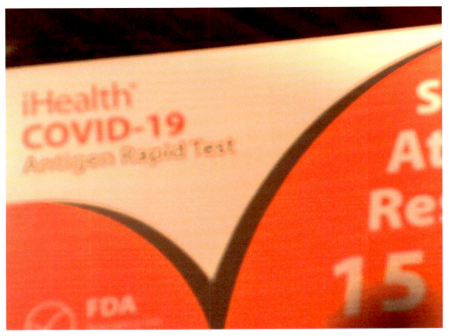

Top Left: I am standing in the hospital entrance remembering being here very sick with COVID. I spent a month at UW Hospital with COVID. I had COVID early in the pandemic, before vaccines. I fully recovered! But needed OT and oxygen at home to help get my strength back.

Top right: Picture of box of at home COVID test. Had to take a test at Whitewater during COVID.

Bottom: People eat their lunch. Tables are spaced out. Helps them to stay apart.

THE PANDEMIC CANCELLED IT, AND THEY NEVER BROUGHT IT BACK

Safety procedure and caution to keep safe from COVID.

I am washing hands. Stay safe and protect from COVID. COVID is serious and real.

Purpose: Keep your hands clean supposed to stop COVID from spreading. Stay away from germs is important.

I'm washing hands. Soap on hands. Killing germs and keeping people safe. Keeping other people safe and not spreading germs around.

Kept my hands clean during the COVID. Keeping the germs away.

Top Left: I am masking up. I mask up around people because I don't know who has COVID. Protect self and following all safety procedures to prevent COVID.

Top right: I'm distancing myself from everything.

Bottom: Protect self and follow all safety procedures to prevent COVID. I'm still doing socially distancing to prevent self from getting COVID.

THE PANDEMIC CANCELLED IT, AND THEY NEVER BROUGHT IT BACK

Me lifting weights and running at my apartment.

They keep my strength up and good for my health. Did during pandemic too. Doing forever. It was important to do during pandemic.

Top Left: Fruit and vegetables, vitamin C and D, helps people get better.

Top right: Aloe vera plant has medicine that helps COVID.

Bottom: I like coffee. I started drinking coffee in the pandemic. You need coffee before you go out to keep from getting sick. I didn't get COVID, but my mom did and I have to take care of her.

THE PANDEMIC CANCELLED IT, AND THEY NEVER BROUGHT IT BACK

ROMANO JOHNSON

My gift was given to me from a golden brown American God. When I was growing up I would go to church and look at the colors. When I think of God, I go to church and I pray, and I ask him to give me ideas and God gives me the gift of drawing in return. I knew that someday my art was going to be enjoyed by everybody around the world. They would love to see my colors and my ideas. Painting is something I've always liked doing. It makes me feel better. It makes me come up with ideas. When I draw and paint I'm always working for better ideas; blending colors, adding glitter, coming up with patterns. I need all of that canvas to communicate all of my ideas. I really love the big size because I have sort of superhero ideas about famous artists and singers. I want people to see that this is what I love doing, and what I always wanted to do.

Romano Johnson—The Yellow Moon Healing God

KARLA AUSDERAU • JENNIFER CAPELLE

Spirituality & Beliefs

Time leads to self-reflection

Prayer

Religious practice

I am appreciating life more. I'm praying. I appreciate God and ability to wake up every day. COVID made me appreciate life more.

Church changed from in person to online. I am showing I am close to God. It is important to get close to God and important in pandemic.

Missed mass because mass had to be done virtually.

Picture of an altar, blessed mother Teresa, St. Francis of Assisi. St. Francis is my name picked for confirmation. I very much like going to mass and it was something that I missed.

I always give my life to God, first thing. I kept myself close to God. Being separated from God is a hard thing.

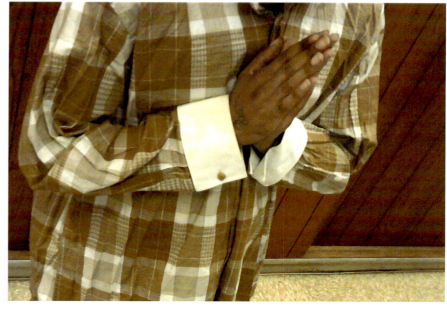

[Praying] helped me stay healthy, sanitizer important. Prayed more during pandemic. Church stayed open during COVID- whole time.

Virtual church on Facebook Live. You get to be there. You can sit at home and watch church. I did this a lot when the pandemic was happening.

Parking lot, trees, at my church. Church is significant. Makes people feel good about themselves. Church was especially important during COVID.

Conclusion

The photos and narratives shared through this research study depict the complex lives of people with intellectual and developmental disabilities and the impact COVID-19 had on their daily lives, disrupting daily routines and community participation. This work contributes to the literature that Photovoice is an exceptional methodology for the inclusion of people with intellectual disabilities in research to elevate and share their lived experiences from a first-hand perspective. In addition, this book emphasizes the importance of inclusive dissemination of research to meet the needs of a broad audience and share the breadth of narratives collected. Thank you for taking the time to engage with the pictures and stories shared by people with intellectual and developmental disabilities during COVID-19.

Hope Land—The Orange Moon

KARLA AUSDERAU • JENNIFER CAPELLE